Copyright © 2020 by Vincent Fuentes

ISBN: 9798653886096

Table of Contents

Those who March

This is not for those
who seek violence
and slaughter,
who spread fear
and hate.

This for those who march
carrying the words of our
dead
and the
dreams of our
children.

For those who stand and sit
facing clubs, cars, and death,
march with those
who marched before.

For being born beautiful
and strong with pride
shout for
"Justice."

You will suffer hate from
the laws and media
who call for your
imprisonment
and death.

The ridicule will haunt your
days and craft your
nightmares.

We're Still Here

Yet, silence the fears
and hatred,
march as a living
testament of love
to harken
change.

Let history record the bravery
of you who march
to give our children
life.

Skin Deep

Every step is the same, ducking and shirking
away from being known as "skin deep."

Can't run away from the birthright of
being blessed/cursed as Black.
echoing of slavery
and
shame.

Those who try to reclaim dignity
are greeted with tombstones
and
disdain.

Where success is seen,
miracles are born
rather than
expected.

You believe in being grateful to
eat scraps,
when all should have
the right to
eat.

Where you
walk unhindered,
guns and slurs
haunt darker footsteps.

Living means one more day
only to wonder if
tomorrow

We're Still Here

you see more than
skin deep.

The Herald

Silence falters against racism
Only inciting people to cry and bleed.

Violence wounds change and spurs progress
or defeat.

If words moved hearts and minds
to action, then war would be no more.

Yet, words are power,
Voices crying as
One to heard.

Tears gas and bullets
are their rewards
for speaking
truth.

Yet, all are slaves to violence.

We refuse to claim this truth, how its power sways
us to change when words falter.

The beckoning of screams
and gunshots
call it forth,

Change.

For ill or good,
It comes hoping for Justice
to be blind no more
and

children to live.

V.M. Fuentes

When will freedom come?

Will it be when we stop breathing?

Will it be when we only speak
when spoken to?

Will it be when our blood
wash your cars and clean your trash?

Isn't it enough that we mark our words
and lower our pride to be
American?

Only when the marching
feet of Negros, Mexicans,
and all people

stand up to the
bullets,
the tear gas
the dogs.

"We want justice!"

Let not the voices of
the dead remain
silent.

People will die in the streets
to join our ancestors
in sacrifice.

Yet, their voices stir our hearts
and urge our feet to march.

We're Still Here

To join our hands in fellowship,
and echoing our
ancestors, mothers, fathers,
sisters, and brothers.

"We want Justice!"

Freedom

Is the right to walk,
to breathe,
to eat,
to speak.

Until a walk down the street
is without sirens,
freedom is lost.

Until struggling to breath
is without crushing,
freedom is stolen.

Until food is without
price,
freedom is far.

Until speaking is heard
without bullets and gas,
freedom is yours.

Until you cease killing skin
voices cry and bleed,
flooding the streets
till it happens

screams turn to laughter,
tears to smiles,
hate to love,
despair to joy,

That is Freedom.

Mute

The softness of "breath" lends itself to being lost
in the struggle of dying.

The resounding CRACK and BANG
only muffle the sounds of
last words.

Living even harder.

Breathing stops as cops
pass by
wondering if living
is today's reward.

Shallow breaths belong to
being stopped and frisked.

Laws are blind to such crimes,
justice and safety steal
breath faster
then sirens.

Beaten until success is measured
in stolen culture and bloody
histories

of who you should be
rather than
who you are...

The Next Generation

To be seen and not heard
is your place for us but
the words from those who have died
echo, immortalized in our
souls.

The freedom of those who cry and bleed
survive through us who kneel
who speak with those who
died.

It's those blood and bones that
fuel our hearts and minds,

yet, it's our tears that
water our Children's
dreams.

Dreams where they can
speak and not be beaten
walk and not be frisked
laugh and not be shot

A dream of being free...

echo

hallowed out of dusty corners
and forgotten closets

i peer through the musty glass
as they walk by, hand in
hand

as if guided by music in
the night.
different

yet, paired in rhythm
and rhyme.

i couldn't see more
behind the cage
where

see me.

Pizza Dinner

It was 5 pm
the pizza was
black around the
edges with

brown cheese.
Taking a slice
to shove in—"Stupid"

"Eat normal." Mom shook
her head, serving
my brother.

"Yes, mom."
I voice
as
the barrage of
boxes
marked: Kitchen, Living Room,
Movies, and

my favorite: Books.
Fortify us.

Weighing a ton
for boys
like me and my brother.

For only $6.99
Mom bought
this burnt
dinner
for our

We're Still Here

1st night

Here.

Here, away
From our childhood
Home, family, and
friends...

raised by a Mom with
bags for eyes
and
growing crow's feet.

Smiling, for an
affordable meal
where my brother
and I ate.

She leaned against
a box or two
as I handed water
to

all, before
saying a silent
prayer,

"Lord, thank you, for not letting dad come home."

no more

cast aside for poison
or cure
or

a brittle concoction
that seethes

death.

coming, running,
past me

as i scream
into the blue
sky,

the pale
moon

"Can you hear me?"

Our allies

aren't those who say "i don't see color."
but are those who step out of a
bus to meet the beastial crowd.

They are the helping hand that
feeds you when you can't
pay a bill.

As you sink beneath darkened
thoughts and razor slices,
they whisper and catch
your hand saying,
"life is worth living."

They are the smiles and hugs
as you brave yourself for
leaving the
closest.

As you scream in fury and sorrow
they come anyway, some
close, others far
there if need be
to give space.

When you tire from the
beatings of yesterday and
tomorrow's the same,

They come healing your
wounds to hold death
and help you to
safety.

V.M. Fuentes

Life is filled with
torture and strife
who's to say a
few allies wouldn't
go a long way.

The shower

let pour the healing water of the world
to wash the blood of the conquered
before you write history
as is the right of victors,
further stealing the voices of
people whose history
is no more.

Come see here, the parchment is skin
and ink blood, tattooed onto this
country fair.

How can one wash in atonement
of past transgressions?

But wait, tarry here for a moment
to listen,
Listen to the murmurs of
those beneath your
shoes and
smell the flowers
blooming in graveyards.

As the pen rushes to quench
thirst and chain those
unworthy of breath,

wait! Wait for a time,
are they really so different?
The conquered and you?
The freedom fighter and
terrorist?

V.M. Fuentes

Which time were one and now
the other?

When were you the slave and
now the master?

Has the water stopped running?
Nay, as dirt and grime lose
to cool waves
the cries are drowned
out by a sigh of
relief.

For they are gone and you
are still standing.

Yet, as you step out of
that shower,
hear the water dripping
and draining.

Reminding you of
how everything is better
than it was,
but is it?

We're Still Here

Though our parents and grandparents
plant your trees,
pick your fruit,
trim your hedges.

We're still here,
tending the land of our
birth, stolen
with blood and false
promises

though we bleed in the streets
where bottle and needle
are medicine,
a vehicle to
escape.

We're still here,
surviving in tents
and chased by
hate

though my family trudged
the path laden with broken
tears and starved children.

We're still here,
scrapping by in relocations
and reservations
wondering how our
ancestors cry

though our fathers and mothers

hung from trees, burned
like crosses while
chains and cuffs shadow
hallow freedom.

We're still here,
catching bullets
and tattoos to
survive only
to die

Though you steal our
children and suffer
them to rape and starvation.

We're still here,
wondering how America
was ever free...

Though we work for hunger
and thirst as you steal
medicine and history.

We're still here,
as you eat cake and
mock us to
"Work harder!"

Though you made our sex
criminal, our gods immoral,
subject to slaughter and ridicule.

We're still here,
loving men, women,
both or none,

27

We're Still Here

Love is more than
Adam & Eve.

We're still here.

V.M. Fuentes

Nothingness

Buzzing round a mound of dung
Left little to the imagination.

Fortune failing and yet again call
To the debts of time.

A taskmaster no kinder than a fisherman
Who baits those saps with delectable
Treats of wealth and paradise.

Such a glamor would fool Solomon
The wise, for he too paid his
Dues to time's coffers.

Nothing is ever kept only lent,
Borrowed from a miser
Who's greed slaughters all.

Yet, it's cousin Death, never fickle
Always tickles those with no
Time to spare.

Young or old,
Rich or poor

To bargain with
Death
For a little time
More.

So tarry hear a moment
More to hear this
Last tale

29

We're Still Here

Of one whose
Reading lines
That never reach
Its finish...

V.M. Fuentes

A lover's feast

Oh, if love were sweets
I'd eat two a day
A tart, a cookie maybe
But never a cake
Or pie.

For what has being sick on love
Ever brought?

To give life and limb,
Food and drink to
One, who's left
Long ago.

Nothing more than a shade
Was she, vapor or morning
Dew.

"Where has she gone?"

"Leave her be!"

Enough cake, stay
This diet of sweeties

And begin to feed on
The like

Remember the haunting cool aid
Of gods and spirits, disguised as wine
To sell cheap tickets to
Paradise.

We're Still Here

Remember the meat of histories
And aged ham that caution
You against drinking wine.

Come, taste the fruits of Justice
Tempered with mercy or
The virtues of morality
That soured long ago.

Perhaps wafers of philosophy
Are more to your liking
If you prefer bland and
Ceaseless musings.

But by all means please
Cease this madness
With love's delicacies
And sweeties.

Banish its honey and chocolate
From your mouth to
Never again

Fall sick
With love's
Crippling disease.

Soulmate

I loved you without
knowing why you're there
or how you came.

I first met you at 26
before I knew what love is.

You never asked why or how
I came by
but
our first kiss
reached farther than
heaven.

But

your touch, filthier
then
Sin.

Oh, how your tongue tasted me
night and day.

Soon we left school for jobs,
minimum wage but
we were happy.
As I yearn for the
wedding of a lifetime

you leave for Prozac Island at 35
and I don't see you.
Till I cheek the pills
and drink our last

bottle.

You show up with
flowers and satin sheets
on a bed with restraints.

You whisper, "I love you."
And taste my flesh,
lips, hips,
my juices,
all me.
But you leave again at 50
and I'm rushed to that
padded prison with
needles and bright
lights,
across the way.

"Why won't you come back?
"Have I done something?"
"Why do you hate me?"

The last time we speak at 62,
my Dr. says, "You're not real."
But he's wrong, you don't look
a day over 26, your hair's
the same cut,
eyes aglow and
skin of gold.
Your name is_____

V.M. Fuentes

Till Death do us part...

I let you have me,
as I cover my flinching
with gasps, feigning orgasm
from your bruising touch.

I let you eat me,
perfect hair, red lips,
and all, till I breathe
in your smile of
Good times.

I let you lie to me,
can't stop or risk
losing hope for
those
empty blue eyes.

I let you see me
the morning after.
Smirking at your handiwork
wondering if I'm
pregnant.

Can't get out...
Baby #2 is on the way,
at least you don't touch
them.
Maybe they'll be
safe?

BANG!

I let you die,

you gasp like I have.
Each time you echo
"Sorry, babe."
My sons cry,
scream,
"Mommy, Daddy!"

Only you reach for them
as I fade from the prison
you sentenced me to
BANG!

Mirage

Sometimes what a person needs isn't
a hug or even the words
"I'm sorry."
But a conscious effort to be
left alone.

To gaze at the dwindling moon
in solace and tears.
Remembering just moments
ago, you wrestled me
to the ground
tore my jeans
while I stared into oblivion.

Even then, to stand apart is
something normal for through
the crowd I wade among
stars and moons.

Finished. You leave only
to be caught smiling with
wolf eyes at school.
As I fade into mom's
pill bottle.

Musings of Wandering

Couldn't bear to be left alone
as trees shorn their leafy
children in the blinking Moon.

Yet, as the soft earth swallows
my feet, I walk towards the
eclipsing horizon.

Passing town after town,
I see the
happiness echoing empty
cradles and
ask
"Will man ever change?"

Roundtrip back home to
her who bore me screaming
but all were away...

Down the pungent alley
I walk, met with frenzied dog
biting at my heels,
whose eyes, bereft of pride,
drip scarlet tears.
"I wish I had a leg to spare."

Next, a boy holding
out a cup with coins
and smiles.
No one notices, but
I do
still, I walk by...

Couldn't believe how iPhones
become IVs,
lifelines to the Now
as none recognize
the wilting rose
or
dying oak.

I see testaments to flesh
as Billboards of Models
pervade the skies
as cars zoom
over their neighbors,
racing to themselves.

Give me forests where
the air smells like
snow music
and
tastes like
honeyed poems.

Let me bathe in
the solitude of
spring rain
where healing,
goodness,
and peace reign.

Stone.

Standing on the steps
of the forest's mouth

I stare at the lush beauty
of towering trees
and fragrant flowers.

None provide solace for
the emptiness within.

A severing of the soul
came from her departure.

In the city, I plaster a smile
of relief, of happiness
masking the sullen

abyss of shattered love.
I laugh at half-hearted jokes
and toast the many years to
come.

Yet, in the barren nights of
empty sheets and frigid beds
I awake,

Gazing at the same moon
you are.

Brilliant in its greying white
like a dull bone
freshly washed from
my

40

corpse.

I cannot see the suffering
in my eyes when I see

your photos.

A smile echoing laughter
Long hair glistening
Skin smoother than glass

is gone.

Bereft of little more
than memories of
us.

All those years ago
decades it was
since you last
said,
"Hey..."

Grief

More so than the sadness and anger
that comes in waves is

the mind-numbing fear
that comes as tumultuous

rivers, to every fiber of
your being.

It's the tingling of your
fingertips.

It's the gnawing at the
back of your head.

It's the twittering whispers
of what if's and should haves

that creep by every minute of
every hour till the sweat
on your brow drives
you mad.

They say, "patience is a virtue."

Yet, this tortuous virtue
is fraught with
disappointment
and shame
for standing still

waiting...

As your feet yearn to trample
obstacles to face the dread
or
simply run and hide
from harrowing
dead.

Goodbye

Skulls abound in pink basinets
as the moon dwindles below.

Where the sun is pushed forth to
settle in the vast clouds in
blue sky.

For they watch untold horrors
and pleasantries that lay waste

To the human race.

Behold! They sit!
Our celestial watchers

As the two-legged ones
hasten the end of earth

With poison in its waters, rivers,
and ponds.

Oh, how those mighty trees were
for industry and waste

that dribbled down or rose in
ash and smoke, choking
the air for profit.

As they eat, drink, and
fight each other to extinction.

These stars of fire and ice
do sit in awe of how

44

hubris decimates the world.

Debtors prison

To think I could repay my
mother with wine and
cards
as if paper and juice
could bypass

shelter in summer,
warmth in winter,
sleep in spring,
fulfillment in fall.

Repayment of my
sister's kindness
with
actionless words
and
a hug or two.

Can these clear the
debts of
logical teachings
and
creative expression?

Yet, as my father
supplies house
and
hearth

does a meager sweeping
and
raking
balance the scales?

Or my friends with
tears a plenty as
they feed me,
clothe me,
guard my heart.

Wherein, I found myself and
the learned of
the world within.

Seeing the path laid bare
I too wish to be decent but all
I am is smoke and mirrors,

given everything, may I be deserving.

Departure

Silence echoes through the building,

though the normative beeping and buzzing
are heard by humans,

none hear the way
my cane thumps the tile
or the ticking of
my watch.

It's been ticking since
before Time itself

was birthed, as if
waiting, watching for
the moment to arrive.

Those foolish mortals do
haste past me, eager

to bargain, desperate to
save. Yet, as

I glance at the child, surrounded
by a mother's tears

buried underneath tubes
and wires.

His eyes open and
smiles beneath the
tube breathing for him.

Despite it all, he asks,
"Is it time to play?"

I nod, reaching to touch
his head as the monitor
beeps.

And the hands on
my watch
reads
4:57

Reaper's Song

Beginning with harrowing cries
a mortal husk leaves
survivors angered, fearful of their
fate.

As his time draws near
he sees his mother
behind steel bars.
She couldn't love him more.

A sullen man plays dress up with
the dead. Painting their faces a
vibrant hue, a pauper's attempt
to mimic life.

I have never felt more
until visiting the gravestones
of my loved ones.
Their love—quivering
and infinite.

Just the way it was supposed to be

Of all the paths in life
I chose this one.

Why?

Oh, I'm sure I could draw you
a picture
Or
paint you a movie.

But that would be a waste,

Why?

It can seem harsh
Or
cruel the way life
comes in
droves

of laughter and tears.

But beneath it all
lives a bewilderment
we don't understand.

I go left,
You go right,

You lead,
I follow.

But in some

We're Still Here

cases we never
see each other.

Take it down,
draw one more,

sing a verse,
eat a feast

utter whispers,
walk alone
in cold
Or
in warmth

Life doesn't judge.

I'm here now
and that's all
I can say.

Maybe next time
it'll be better,
for worse is the
stuff of nightmares
but sometimes
that happens
too

V.M. Fuentes

Foggy window

Do you hear it?
the faint pitter patter
of rain

smashed across the glass.
Its vehicle, a fearsome
gale

that wrenches trees
and whips branches
only to shoot down leaves.

Yet, the blissful slithering
of ice blue lightning
brings peace.

Often succeeded
by thunderous applause
as it arcs and twists

beyond what light should
do.

Still bloom

as water shoots down
then calms down
it comes.

Ruby petals and vermilion fridges
burst under the gentle
rain
and
harsh gale.

Instead of retreating
this persists
and
thrives
to yet again

bring fire to the
haze of
grey
and
white.

From a thinning green
fountain it grows
among hairy
leaves
and
stout branch.

Only to bloom
for the rain,
joyful,

V.M. Fuentes

it dances

with water to
lead
and
petals
to follow.

The melancholy
clouds
and
whistling winds
beckon
them

to dance
to the music
of change.

Spectre

"Look! In the mirror!"
I said.

There I stood besotted with that horrid figure
who croaked and wheezed,
trapped in glass
daring to scrape and scratch.

Did I marvel?
Did I wonder?
At who this figure tried
to snatch and bite,
trapped in glass
still scarcely dare I
muttered,

"What are you?"

Craning its neck as pus drip drip drip
into a hole,
what hole? I know not for
how can one see past the
glass?

Then the air grew thin, swallowing my last breath
to pave the way for a fragrance that
beckoned the shadow of her
that left such a soul in
sorrow-trapped in glass.

"Foul beast, leave me! Leave to my
despair that you should dare to
remind me!"

Yet, the figure whose eyes did steel against
my ravings only answered with
a smile.
Haunting and crimson like the
fading roses on my coffin.

"But I can't be dead!"

And it laughed! A screech from the
bowels of the abyss did hiss
setting my teeth to chatter,
skin to shiver,
and heart to still its hasty
beating.

Then it tapped, tapped the glass
with prolonged fingernails
jaundiced and chipped.

It whispered,
"Leave..."

"Yes! Leave, leave me! Beast of hell
sent to haunt me like some
spectre lost!"

But I could see how those fingernails scrape and
scratch at the glass. Then did my soul flutter

at the cracked glass. Only to answer its
cracking, I sent a chorus of silence
to meet the fiend for my legs
had lost their strength
and urgency—rooting me
to face my destiny

as the sickly finger
pressed, pressed
against the
glass.

This mirror shredded the finger,
fingers, now hand reaching
through as pus
burst from frayed
veins
catching my throat,
hands limp,
mouth dry
to say,

"Leave."

Yet, in the jagged glass atop
the mirror did I see
a radiant maiden
whose amber tresses
sat aglow to
give way to
eyes, eyes
of a storm
that could quell
darkness.

There I stood, without totem
or token to banish
the figure back.

When the tapping
came and rain did she
summon to cleanse

the horror that
spilled into my
room.

However, it did not move
only smiled its black
green teeth
hissing its spittle
across my face
and dare I
say more
but this be
my last words,

"Dear heart-"

Darkness clouded, doubtless it
was those fingernails that
did constrict my throat
till breath was
scarcely needed to
keep me from
seeing those
blue grey
eyes
that once spoke
of loving
souls.

But if only I knew

the house was tickled by the fancy of
midnight footsteps on the cold
tile,

limestone, I believe it was.

I couldn't have been more than
12? 13 maybe?

But none of anything mattered
as the house shook from the
gentle breeze

as fog formed on the corners
of the kitchen windows.

The moon summoned shadows to
dance with me down the halls
and up the stairs.

Yet, those that barred my room
were of a pernicious sort
and wholly felt I
needn't be permitted
my bed.

As I placed a hand on the door-
Nothing.

A bleak abyss greeted me like
some spectre sent from
Hades, himself, to
tuck me in.

The blanket was just as cold
as the kitchen tile
I shouldn't wonder
since the window
was ajar.

By whom was answered
in the breeze that
shuttered the window
as the mirror
bounced on the wall.

There! In the chasm of polished
glass sat churlish face
of one hovering
above my
bed.

Bespectacled with scarlet eyes
and jaundiced teeth
to match its
slithering tongue.

If only I had stayed in
the halls, where
the shadows danced
with me!

Or on the limestone
tiles, where my
body lays
on a most chilling
grave
with only dew

for company
instead of demons.

Pursuit

Isn't it enough to say "goodbye?"
Must I listen to the hows and whys
by yesteryear, begging me to stay
yet another day, another hour,
just a moment more...

To be seen
To be heard

Only to fade into sunlight
and travel across the horizon
to be Me.

V.M. Fuentes

The Return

Be still Mr. Clock as your indefinite clanging
does haunt my step.

Ever ringing and ever clanging.

As it strikes 15 going on 20, there is
a painted lady that streaks past to
chase me,

down the nights and the days while
the quivering, dithering echo of
shadows past
do flaunt
themselves

In the daylight, when any respectable
shadow should flee but in
the moonlight...ever in
the moonlight

does it come.

I fled it!

But. It comes in waves
and songs of yesteryear
that plague my soul
with ill repute
and
a manner to shame
sailors.

I fled it!

We're Still Here

Never have my feet carried
this husk on so far
an escape
that would rival
Dante's traveling
to the bowels of Hell
and Heaven.

It was then the mirror caught me
to see what I hadn't or couldn't
I was crying.

Wagon wheels

they twirl and dance around your hands and arms,
abandoning the

wayside for fertile grounds. Where poison
and venom sprout between the budding

sidewalk. Of concrete and dried skeletons
form the steady grey paths leading only deeper and

deeper to the bowels of Hell. To join Orpheus and
Dante on their wayward journeys

that befouled all that was holy and
pure for

those who knew not what time could do.
Of here and there is Life and Death,

two parts like Janus. Same coin
different face:
A Babe,
A Ghoul.

In the mirror I see neither as
the coin ripples through the air

dancing on the first breath
and
swallowing the last ones.

Where do they go, none can say, but
perhaps there's more

We're Still Here

to be said when one
is nothing more than

a breath of fresh air.

Disbelief

The pitter patter of the rain slid down the window like nails on chalkboard. As the rain continued its barrage, I lay in bed. Eyes shut. Ears trembling from the scraping droplets that save none and torture all.

"Is it here? Have you come?"

A creek echoed, foretelling such a creature of vile that I could not seek even in my darkest abysmal dreams. Myths are silent and sacred texts only speak of it in whispers,

careful not to awaken It.

This fearful and dreadful doubting did set my heart a throbbing ever robbing my soul of serene bliss from the Sandman.

But not so, I pull the blanket over my head till a tuft of brown lays still while the walls moan from the wind's harsh handling.

The rain spat on the window, pouring its anger and deceit onto it. For every time it slowed, hope rose from its unsightly grave only to be crushed by watery fervor.

Regardless, my eyes peeked out, fireflies in the night that cower for the air is silent and the night is Its kingdom of shadow and bone...

Then a dash of pink splatters my window, then another and another! Blood poured from the sky, sealing away those hopeful stars and graceful moonlight.

We're Still Here

Tugging the blanket and sheet, slowly ever so as I wait to see it. My eyes bounce hither and thither, but It escapes me!

Only the window reveals my salvation, should I be saved and crash through the seething glass as Its teeth seek to fray muscle and crunch bone?

But where is It?

A stray branch taps the glass, begging me to let in something horrid or angelic, I know not. For the shadow of It fills the room with the stench of suffering that smells no more lovely than a fresh grave.

Yet, there far away from the window if I could see it, lay a streetlight that shone beneath the crimson tempest.

Teasing, entreating me to sever my wrists and lace my arms with blood unborne from peace and let the darkness burrow further than a soul can manage.

V.M. Fuentes

Hooverville

were those of rats and trash live,
they were humans once
lively, laughing, and smiling
some of them.

others couldn't bear to the leave
the sight of things, whether
beatings or
rapes or
worse.

but they're there. Creeping through the
streets,

it's the smell that get you first then
you hear them,

the jingle jangle of
coins,
clanking of carts
and perhaps barking
or two
from dogs.

sometimes friendlier
than most
but!

it came,
batten down the hatches
prescribe toilet paper
and weed
for the everlasting night

We're Still Here

full of exile
and pain.

they were human once
only sin was to be
born in a different class
or by bad luck

but soon they were wheeled and
huddled into overshot shelters
amid the crisis
bartering for
life
as everyone
left.

scraping for food as cities empty
and streets turn green
but they stay
the same,
invisible,
left to their own devices

they call it tent city these days...

V.M. Fuentes

I'm human too

They took my mama from me
till I wandered into the street
to kiss the concrete
as the truck rolled over
me.

I'm human too.

ICE rolled up to collect the "Non-Essentials"
while I'm told to work, to pick
food for those who couldn't care
less.
As I get paid less for you to eat.

I'm human too.

Fighting a war as cannon fodder
while the rich profit from
my blood.
Came and went from a place
not my own.
Firing a gun cause they told me
duty over life.

I'm human too.

Born from farm workers and
orange pickers to graduate
college first.
Only to be called
"illegal" instead of "Dr."

I'm human too.

71

We're Still Here

Sitting beneath bridges and hauling
ass, dodging rocks and bullets
sirens and screams.
As the voices in my
head say,

"We're human too."

Mama and Papa loved me
but were hunted for it.
A crime to be born in mixed skin
where i don't know the language.

I'm human too.

My father's a rapist, now ma can't
look at me now.
Try and try to say, "hi"
She doesn't even hear me.

I'm human too.

The closet can't hold us
but it's walls are safer than
the beatings, stabbings and
bullet holes from being
me.

I'm human too.

A Memoir of Loss

Beneath the rafters, I laid in wait till a time
would arise as I look to gaze at the subtle
surprise of strawberry lemonade in the
clouds.

Oh, to lose a brother or sister or lovers be
that which most can't contend for a loss
none can conceive.

Can't you see the dusk of blue midnight
that wisped far away and through an air of past
doubts and fears, hopes and dreams.

"Begone for you have beguiled me to
naught of worth, I'd wager you were
behind the death of them who I lost."

Perish the thought of recklessness and
obscurity only to forsake the love of them who
bore my soul beneath stars of light.

Better than a doctrine of wails and rules
that would seem to squash the very notion
of memory.

"Move on." They say. "It'll get better soon..." but
be that as it may, grief follows quicker than death
devoid of sleep or pause.

How then shall I be close again to the rain?
Where I showered and drank
my fill of nectar and mist.

We're Still Here

Tarry for a moment and no more but be worth
it evermore and set my soul to fly
in the sun, beneath the clouds.

V.M. Fuentes

Strawberry Lemonade

It's not the color I remember most,
not those swirls of golden rubies

nor the sweeter taste of wilder honey
among sliced strawberries.

But the blush of your lips,
the solitude of your amber eyes

that gave me pause as the glass
grew slick with iced memoirs.

No, it wasn't how you dumped a
spot of sugar or two in my glass.

Only the quiver of your breast
beneath my breath that staved

off hunger and delight. For
madness was common with

every pour and pondering ever
wandering were mine eyes.

Who were weak with lusting
after a glass

of your cool strawberry
lemonade...

The mailman

bending down to deliver today's post
drafty air pulling at his cap

but not wasted by a hand to restrain it
as he stopped just short of

the usual route. Wonder what crossed
his mind as those feet scurried

past, voice trembling at the
inhabitant of plot 119.

Tears watered the grass beyond
the stone as its haunting gaze

beckoned him with those words,
"Cherished Daughter."

The parcel passed from hand to
hand only to be misplaced,

at the next stone
marked, "Beloved Mother."

V.M. Fuentes

First light

her yellowed teeth brightened that lovely smile,
mirroring the stars

that night. Took me a while to notice since
the door creaked like a damn horror movie.

Before coming over, I tried every number
house, cell, even Burger King where you
worked.

Couldn't be reached on a sunday afternoon,
odd but it's not like that

voice would lie. Especially after repeating
over and over, "the number you are

trying to call has been disconnected."
Slipped in the backdoor like last time

before your dad caught us in your bed.
Never ran faster in my life, least

that's what you said when you chucked
my clothes out the window.

Still, sorry I didn't reach you in time
the only day you ever needed

someone to listen, I couldn't be bothered.
Entering your room, I expected you to be

sleeping naked per usual. Till the
mirror shocked me into now-

77

We're Still Here

a lidless corpse hung in the closet.
Echoing that smile who watched

me sleep.

Memento

I sometimes taste you in the bloom of Aster
and smell your fragrance in raspberries.

Oh, the way the moon smiles
carries well wishes and love past.

Till only the sun chases away the
shadow of time and the suffering
beneath.

A picture of you has me believe
we're real as the parting glance
stuns the reality of your absence.

Haunting my mirror are those
ever blue eyes, dazzling like starlight.

That smile and tongue of you,
tantalizing and unquenching,

devoid of color unless in my
dreams...

Ravenous

I crave the taste behind your
ears, enticing my tongue further
tracing down your jaw

to your neck.
Hidden by raven tresses
where your fragrance enchants me.

I crave the afterglow of your skin,
the way it shimmers in summer
and glistens in the rain.

As the east wind
elicit shivers that tickle your
back, trailing to your toes
that curl beneath my breath.

The ease of your shoulders
curve round, guiding my hands
down your chest,
under your breasts,
over your hips.

That I could devour you,
savoring each delicacy of
flesh offered.

Tasting the beads of sweat
as my hands explore the
length of your legs
and feet.

Brushing my lips against

the curve of your ankles,
soothing your breath with
a finger on
honey lips.

Enchant me with eyes
of twilit winters
and
caresses of autumn
to further enflame
my love.

Previously

Amidst this torrid night,
I wonder how the delicacies of
yesteryear have vanished.

A drive across town
wind rustling through
your hair as the songs of
birds outrank the radio.

Or the quaint gathering of friends
on an eve quite like this
where laughter and cheer
are all the rage
and sadness is
banished.

The headlines brought
misery and pain only
cause they were far away
or too close to feel.

Lately, these thoughts overwhelm
me, for how could the world
change faster than a SNAP?

Exiled from meeting in hallowed
halls to preach or pray.

Sequestered from touch and
family squabbles, even those
seem less dismal than
here,

V.M. Fuentes

Surrounded by four walls,
where I'm left to rot
amidst the sorrow for
yesteryear.

Could have been among those
who crave the crashing of waves
or the blaring sirens of music
to dance and wave.

Yet, here we are still to cease all
knowledge of the adversary
who slips and creeps about
the wind, over doorknobs,
and car keys.

Plaguing us with masks to placate
our fear while the bodies
burn in graves reminiscent
of times past.

How quickly did the flame eat
their flesh and cloth.
Spitting ash to the ground
as tears flood from
those too far to see.

It's chow time in the halls
of concrete and bars.
Where I shall be buried
in flames
never remembering the day
I could once more.

"You're doing it wrong."

"Not like this, like this."
she whispered,
taking the razor
slicing her arm from
wrist to elbow
before throwing it at my feet.

it bounced, slicing my big toe
blood pooled
invading the rug,

i admire my Picasso
as my life drained out
marveling as the dark
crimson lines bomb
the rug.

my ears transfixed
by the siren's call
facing the mirror,
i see Mother's gaunt eyes,
that haunt my shadows.

spitting in my face
as if i were a stray.

i didn't whine this time
as it splattered against my
cheek,

"you're Worthless."
slapping me back to
the mirror that held

my face, my Father's face.
Mother cursed me with those words,

"you're Worthless."

since she died nine years ago.

6 AM

I can't breathe...the pressure building in the
bowels of my chest settle on my lungs.
a weighty anvil to hold me fast like
Mjolnir, none can lift it, not even me.

Breathing is taxing, I can't lift it, struggling
to find air as my nose clogs the way
and mouth won't obey.

Sealed with a curse of the mind—stay
Never leave again. Never breathe again.

My heart beats for air that will never
come, it slows for death.

Betrayed by birth as muscles remain transfixed
to the curse's demands of hindering my
breath.

My tongue blocks life, in or out, it
Won't let me breathe! Come back!

Forcing breathe out can't come sooner for
nothing feels as refreshing as
springtime but
still my eyes droop
and limbs feel like stones.

Swimming through tar, can't escape my
bed, where can I go to break this curse?

Yet, as my phone cries 5 past 6 AM,

V.M. Fuentes

"My God...it's only been five minutes..."

6 feet

It's the space you take, my space, your space

away from me and no closer,
but here and now,

if i could only touch you again

the warmth of your lips
hidden behind that mask.

the smell of your hair,
bundled away.

It wasn't here, where we could stay
but no closer than in earshot.

"I'm sorry, just not today."

If you were any farther, it wouldn't work
but in that golden space lies

the ticket to safe happiness,
tainted by the mask
that hides your smile.

till then be safe, carry on
surrounded by four walls
and the silence of your mind.

it shakes the soul of you
and can't be more than
the world who

shout and scamper about
like rats or mice,

trying to see where we left off
and where we should go.

It's here and no more,

6 feet, not an inch more.

Modern World

Let those whose terror grip them in a vise
cast away the shackles of despair and worry
to meet another day head on.

Allow the lurking shadows to eclipse the flaming
tendril within a soul and see one fade into oblivion.

Yet, as the flame smolders it brightens even
amidst the coming carrion and spectres
seeking those sheltered in place.

Though the walls imprison and restrict,
only those who look out the window
can see more than a room.

A portal to the world beyond where masks
are scarce and guns are coming.

Even then butterflies come and
hummingbirds sing and
squirrels collect.

For as sure as the sun sets
and moon comes,
the ever glistening horizon
reminds the world,
light is where the
shadows are darkest
and gloom pervades the
air.

V.M. Fuentes

In Transit

Beneath azure waves
a body is enveloped

as diamond spheres
escape from noiseless

mouth...

pop, pop echo through
an entrapped brain.

Fruitless arms flail as
legs spasm,

slip into
carnivorous depths.

Crimson evicts vapors
to mingle with waves

as shadows encroach
upon faint blue hue.

Bliss

Pink petals drown beneath
a breeze of

blossoms...emerge from
a wooden arm.

As the tree sings
it sways with the sun.

Facade

They ebb and flow underneath
cascading stars

Between twilight glances
of azure and burgundy

as pink mist envelopes
cracked marble.

Alone

My eyes race against my heart,
Eyelids fluttering thrash my body,
Fear creeping in my bones.

Its spectral eyes haunt my dreams,
Chase my heart to the abyss.

Standing at the precipice, ready to
Bask in the dark emptiness,
Outshining the blistering sun.

White walls call me home
As tear stained pillows
Reek of loneliness.

The scratchy fibers curse my skin,
It wasn't there that I tried to sleep
Rather the shambles of clean clothes
Littered across my sheets.

Waning Moon

Night enveloped him as stars shone,
only wind accompanied him then.

Before long a snowy owl hooted
against stars of a different sort.

No moon to light his way,
he breathed in nature's time—

the owl glided, seeking dinner.
A tear kissed the ground beneath

his boots. It would have been
nice to see her again before his time.

He gulped multicolored pills
upon reaching the summit.

The owl flew past him
while he caught a stone,

deciding it should be
beneath the sky

instead of hidden away
beside lint and dust.